CATHOLIC IMMIGRANTS
IN THEIR SHOES

BY JEANNE MARIE FORD

Published by The Child's World®
1980 Lookout Drive • Mankato, MN 56003-1705
800-599-READ • www.childsworld.com

Content Consultant: William Hal Gorby, PhD, Teaching Assistant Professor, West
Virginia University

Photographs ©: Shooting Star Studio/Shutterstock Images, cover, 1; Hulton Archive/
Getty Images, 6; North Wind Picture Archives, 8; iStockphoto, 9; Everett Historical/
Shutterstock Images, 10, 13, 18, 19; akg-images/Newscom, 14, 16; Osorio/AP Images,
20; AP Images, 22, 24, 25; Shutterstock Images, 26; Red Line Editorial, 28

ISBN 9781503827943
LCCN 2018944109

Printed in the United States of America
PA02394

ABOUT THE AUTHOR

Jeanne Marie Ford is an Emmy-winning TV scriptwriter who holds a master of
fine arts degree in writing for children from Vermont College. She has written
numerous children's books and articles. Ford also teaches college English.
She lives in Maryland with her husband and two children.

TABLE OF CONTENTS

FAST FACTS

Who Are Catholics?

- The head of the Catholic Church is the Pope.
- Catholics had become the largest religious group in the United States by 1906. However, in 2017 Catholics were no longer the largest religious group.

Who Are Protestants?

- The Protestant **Reformation** began in 1517 AD with a German monk named Martin Luther. Luther objected to certain Catholic beliefs and practices. These included praying to the saints and obeying the Pope.
- After splitting from the Catholic Church, Protestants formed many different **denominations**. These included Anglicans, Lutherans, and Baptists, among many others.

Conflict Between Catholics and Protestants

- Most American colonists were Protestant. Although they shared a Christian faith and many beliefs with the Catholics, they did not think religious freedom should extend to Catholics.

TIMELINE

1845–1855: More than 1.5 million people move to the United States from Ireland. Nearly one million Germans come to the United States. Most of the Irish immigrants and about one-half of the Germans are Catholic.

1848: The United States acquires land from Mexico, making approximately 80,000 Mexicans U.S. citizens. The majority of these Mexican Americans are Catholic.

1854: The Know-Nothing party scores major Congressional election wins. This party is strongly anti-Catholic.

1880–1924: Four million Italians come to the United States. Most of them are Catholic.

1890–1920: Two million Polish-speaking people come to the United States. Many of them are Catholic.

1942–1964: The Bracero Program encourages Mexican **migrants** to work in the United States. Many of them are Catholic.

1959: Many Catholic Cubans flee to Florida as **refugees**.

Chapter 1

COLONIAL CATHOLICS

A giant bonfire lit up the autumn sky one night in the 1760s. Men and boys crowded around a stage pulled by horses. On it stood a likeness of the Pope. Beside it was an **effigy** of the devil. The colonists who had gathered chanted insults about their Catholic neighbors. Two masked men swooped in and set the effigies on fire. The people cheered.

Many colonial towns observed Pope Day every year. In Britain, the holiday was called Guy Fawkes Day. It celebrated the defeat of a Catholic man who had tried to murder King James I. The Pope had had nothing to do with Fawkes's scheme. However, many American colonists were filled with hatred for the Pope and his followers. The colonists were afraid that French Catholics might invade from nearby Canada and force their religion on them.

Catholic citizens often lived in fear. In the late 1600s, Catholic immigrant Ann Glover was put on trial in Boston, Massachusetts. When asked to recite the Lord's Prayer, Glover spoke in a mixture of Latin and her native Irish Gaelic language. Witnesses decided she was possessed. The crowd jeered as she was hanged for alleged witchcraft. Her death was a warning to other Catholics that they, too, might be harmed for practicing their faith.

Some colonies were more tolerant of Catholics than others. Maryland was founded by a Catholic named Cecil Calvert. He wanted all Christians to live together peacefully. But Calvert told his fellow Catholics that "all acts of Roman Catholic worship" should be done "as privately as may be."[1] That's because he could not guarantee freedom of religion for Maryland Catholics.

Protestant lawmakers in Maryland passed laws to make it difficult for Catholics to worship. They were not allowed to become teachers or lawyers. When they tried to vote, they were asked to take oaths against their faith.

In the 1760s, anti-Catholic feelings were at an all-time high. However, that changed during the Revolutionary War (1775–1783).

▲ **Cecil Calvert was born in 1605.**

▲ **The Declaration of Independence was signed in 1776.**

The colonists needed the Catholics' help to fight against Britain. On November 5, 1775, George Washington forbade Pope Day celebrations. By the time the colonists won their independence, hatred toward Catholics had lessened. Freedom of religion was guaranteed in the Bill of Rights of the new government.

The Catholic minority in the United States enjoyed relative peace for several decades. But soon, massive waves of Catholic immigrants from Europe would reignite the flames of hatred.

Chapter 2

IRISH AND GERMAN CATHOLICS

Ireland's grassy fields are so green that the country is known as the Emerald Isle. However, beneath the rich soil in 1845, a fungus attacked the potato crops, turning the roots into reddish-brown goo. The Irish people depended on potatoes to survive. They ate them for breakfast, lunch, and dinner. The average man consumed 14 pounds (6.4 kg) of potatoes every day.

Farmers sprinkled holy water on their fields and prayed their crops would grow. Yet for seven years straight, the Irish people starved. Between 1845 and 1852, nearly one million people died. This period was known as the potato **famine**.

Millions of Irish people escaped starvation by leaving their homeland. They scraped together their last pennies to buy passage on ships. The voyage to the United States took four weeks. The passengers were herded together below deck. The air was stale and dank. Each adult had barely enough room to turn around. So many people died that the boats were known as coffin ships.

Traveling on a ship was difficult for many people. One passenger stood at the ship's rail. One of his hands clutched the rail and he held the other hand to his stomach. Waves pushed against the ship and made it sway from side to side. He tried to fight the seasickness, but he threw up into the dark water below.

After weeks at sea, the passenger made it safely to the United States. But like most Irish immigrants, he was poor and many people disliked him because he was Catholic. Many Americans regarded Catholics as stupid, dirty, and lazy. They believed that immigrants took away jobs from American workers.

They turned away job applicants with signs that read, "No Irish Need Apply."[2]

The potato famine also affected crops in the state of Bavaria in Germany. Residents there also suffered from hunger. At the same time, political revolutions in 1848 caused many Germans to leave their homeland. Of the more than one million Germans who immigrated to the United States in the mid-1800s, about one-half were Catholic.

Although most Irish Americans settled in poor slums in the cities where they landed, many German immigrants had enough money to move west. They made new homes in rural Midwestern communities. Because they tended to have more education and money than Irish immigrants, they experienced less **discrimination**.

In the 1850s, a political party called the Know-Nothings gained power in many cities and states. The Know-Nothings believed that Catholic values were not American values. In 1854, a mob in Maine dragged a Catholic priest into the street. The priest cried for help, but none came. His eyes widened in horror as the mob tore off his clothes. They covered him in hot tar and feathers.

A year later, Know-Nothing members guarded polling places to keep Catholics away on election day in Louisville, Kentucky.

▲ **Northern states and Southern states fought against each other during the Civil War.**

They brawled in the streets with German and Irish Catholic immigrants. Between 20 and 100 immigrants died in the fighting on this day in Louisville. It became known as Bloody Monday.

By 1861, the United States was torn apart by the Civil War (1861–1865). Hundreds of thousands of Irish and German immigrants signed up to fight. In spilling their blood for their country, they won respect and acceptance from their fellow Americans, at least for a time.

Chapter 3

SOUTHERN AND EASTERN EUROPEAN CATHOLICS

Paulina Caramando's earliest memories held images of the cobblestone streets of her town in Southern Italy. She remembered the clay jugs the women used to carry water. She remembered piles of oranges and olives being shaken from trees.

◄ **Millions of Italian immigrants were taken to Ellis Island once they arrived in the United States.**

Paulina was eight years old when her family made the voyage to the United States in 1920. She had to leave behind nearly everything, even her doll. The passage on the steamship took 22 days. The bitter smell of coffee on board turned her stomach. Finally, the ship reached New York Harbor. After her family left the ship, Paulina looked on in wonder as her father bought a bright yellow piece of fruit from a vendor. Until then, she had never seen a banana.

As they disembarked on Ellis Island, the women and children were separated from the men. They waited in long lines and stripped off their clothes to be disinfected. Doctors peered into their eyes and throats and asked dozens of questions. Paulina did her best to look healthy and alert so she would not be turned away.

"I came to America because I heard the streets were paved with gold. When I got here, I found out three things. First, the streets were not paved with gold. Second, they weren't paved at all. Third, I was expected to pave them."[3]

—*Italian immigrant, Ellis Island Museum*

Paulina's family settled in Massachusetts, where her father worked for the railroad. Paulina grew up and married an Italian immigrant. They had two sons. One of them died of cancer. Paulina and her husband later divorced. She remarried a farmer, who had two sons of his own. Though her life in the United States was far from easy, Paulina was grateful for what she did have.

During World War II (1939–1945), a bomb ripped through Paulina's childhood home in Italy. "I always say thank God my father decided to come here," Paulina said about the United States.[4] Otherwise, her whole family could have been killed.

▲ **Many Italian families were hopeful that they would have better lives in the United States.**

Between 1880 and 1920, four million Italians came to the United States. Like the Irish, many were fleeing **poverty**. In 1871, separate areas of Italy had unified. In Southern Italy, taxes increased, but living conditions grew worse. Many young men left to find work in the United States.

Many Italian immigrants settled in East Coast cities such as New York City and Philadelphia, Pennsylvania. Sometimes a whole Italian village would move to the same city block. They continued many of their customs from home, such as ringing church bells and hosting lavish weddings and baptisms. They also held colorful parades.

At the turn of the century, immigrants also poured in from Eastern European countries. One place they came from was Poland. Similar to the Italians, they preserved their culture and Catholic faith. Beginning in 1884, Catholic schools had begun cropping up across the United States to teach Catholic culture and values.

The Cyberts family lived in western Pennsylvania. Their town had a Polish Catholic school in one neighborhood, an Irish Catholic school in another, and a Slavic Catholic school in yet another. At the Polish school the Cyberts children attended, the students spoke Polish. They learned Polish history and prayers. They hung out after school at the Polish social club.

They also listened to Polish music. In contrast, students in public schools read the Protestant version of the Bible. They were assigned anti-Catholic literature to read.

Some Americans were wary of the most recent Catholic immigrants. Many immigrants had darker skin than the northern Europeans who had come before them. Immigration laws dating to the 1700s granted citizenship to "free white persons" of "good moral character."[5] Some people were not sure the newest immigrants qualified.

▲ **Some Italian immigrants lived in poverty after coming to the United States.**

▲ **Millions of Europeans fled their homes during the World Wars.**

Until the 1880s, the United States had welcomed nearly everyone who wanted to enter. But then Congress began passing laws to keep out people it considered undesirable. Beginning in 1917, immigrants were required to pass a reading test. In 1921 and 1924, strict **quotas** were passed to limit immigrants from nations outside of northern Europe.

During World War I (1914–1918), many immigrants fought bravely for the United States. Discrimination against Italian and Polish immigrants gradually decreased as the next generation adjusted to life in the United States.

Chapter 4

SPANISH-SPEAKING CATHOLICS

Julio Menocal's family found a tiny patch of shade beneath a mesquite tree. They were in Mexico's Sonoran Desert. It was a hot January day in 1964. Julio tried not to look at the skull of a dead animal that lay nearby. After they'd eaten the last of their food, the Menocals piled back into their car and resumed their journey from Mexico to the United States.

Julio's father drove past a gas station. He had carefully calculated that he had enough fuel in his tank to make it to the next one. But the next gas station was closed. Now Julio was afraid they wouldn't make it. At the top of every crest in the road, his father turned off the ignition. The car coasted downhill. When it sputtered to a stop, he turned the key again.

At last, they reached the Texas border. The children were sweaty and thirsty. Julio's mother told them to wade into a small pond nearby with their clothes on. A cow standing on the bank extended its long tongue to lick sweat off Julio's brother's head.

Unlike the Menocals, the first Mexican Americans never had to cross a border. In 1848, land in what is now Texas, Arizona, New Mexico, and California became part of the United States after the Mexican-American War (1846–1848). Tens of thousands of Mexican citizens, the majority of them Catholic, became Americans overnight.

During the 1800s, many immigrants walked for days across the hot desert to cross the Mexican-American border. Limits on immigration did not apply to them because U.S. farmers depended on Mexican workers. In the 1930s, the U.S. economy crashed. Then, the U.S. government forced Mexicans to leave.

▲ **In 1951, border patrol inspectors fingerprinted undocumented Mexican immigrants before sending them back to Mexico.**

The government wanted to save jobs for U.S. workers. But a decade later, Americans needed Mexican labor during World War II. The Bracero Program, which ran from 1942 to 1964, encouraged Mexican migrants to work on U.S. farms.

Though the pay was meager and the working conditions were poor, more than five million Mexicans came.

Spanish-speaking Catholics also immigrated to the United States from other countries. In 1898, Puerto Rico became a U.S. territory. Between 1945 and 1960, one million Puerto Ricans moved to the mainland in search of better job opportunities. In 1959, many refugees from Cuba fled a revolution. They boarded makeshift rafts and made a treacherous journey to Florida.

By 1950, many white American Catholics had reached the middle class. They no longer felt unwelcome. In 1960, Americans even elected the first Catholic president, John F. Kennedy, who was of Irish descent. Yet many Latino Catholics were not welcomed in existing American churches. The Latino Catholics built their own parish communities that preserved their language and worship traditions. They also turned Catholic social teaching into action as they fought for the rights of the poor.

"As an immigrant, I appreciate, far more than the average American, the liberties we have in this country."[6]

—Gloria Estefan, Cuban American singer

▲ **Braceros harvested crops on California farms.**

In 1965, Congress passed the Hart-Celler Act. It limited immigration from countries in the western hemisphere. This included Latin American countries. Julio understood how lucky he was to have been a legal immigrant just before the Hart-Celler Act was passed. After attending medical school, he opened a clinic to serve poor and immigrant children.

◄ **Mexican workers were used by employers as cheap labor during the Bracero Program.**

Chapter 5

GLOBAL CATHOLICS

I n 1987, Ailsa Fitzwilliam sat in the U.S. Embassy in Trinidad and Tobago—an island country near Venezuela. She was overwhelmed by a thick college catalog. She knew she wanted to leave her developing nation in search of better opportunities in the United States. She applied to Johns Hopkins University in Maryland because it had a program in the engineering major she wanted to pursue.

◄ **People of the Catholic faith can be from any background.**

The school's Catholic community reached out to her before she arrived and later helped her adjust to college life in the United States. No matter how busy Fitzwilliam was, she wanted to go to Mass daily.

Fitzwilliam later met Flavio Mendéz. They got married and had a daughter, Leia-Sofía, in 2001. Fitzwilliam's heart swelled with pride as a crown of flowers was placed on Leia-Sofía's head at her Catholic school graduation. Leia-Sofía was a modern American Catholic. She was also a child of immigrants and was raised in a community with traditions from many different origins.

Today, Masses in the United States are celebrated in Spanish, Vietnamese, and the Filipino language, Tagalog.

"I grew up in a family where my dad wasn't Catholic. But he still went to church every day. We were very religious from that perspective. Flavio coming from a broken home wasn't quite that way. He said early on in our marriage when Leia-Sofía was an infant how important it was for him to go to Mass because he wanted that example for her."[7]

—Ailsa Fitzwilliam

RELIGIONS IN THE UNITED STATES

People practice many religions in the United States. In 2017, Catholics made up approximately 22.7 percent of the U.S. population.

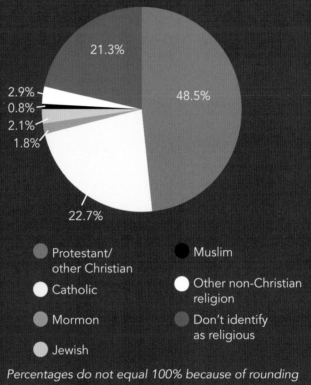

21.3%

2.9%
0.8%
2.1%
1.8%

48.5%

22.7%

- Protestant/other Christian
- Catholic
- Mormon
- Jewish
- Muslim
- Other non-Christian religion
- Don't identify as religious

Percentages do not equal 100% because of rounding

However, despite the United States' rich immigrant heritage, public feelings against immigrants were on the rise in the 2000s.

Pope Francis sent a message to the United States in 2017. "Continue dreaming," he told young immigrants in the country.

"Take care of the country that welcomes you; accept and respect its laws and walk together along that path of love." He reminded Americans that the Bible commanded them to care for migrants. "Jesus, too, was a refugee," he said.[8]

THINK ABOUT IT

- Why do you think Catholics have gained greater acceptance in U.S. society over time?
- Can you think of other religious or ethnic groups that have experienced discrimination in the United States? Explain why they're discriminated against.
- Do you think immigration laws that target certain religious or ethnic groups are fair? Explain your answer.

GLOSSARY

denominations (dih-nah-muh-NAY-shuns): Different branches of the Protestant Church are called denominations. Protestant denominations include Baptists and Lutherans.

discrimination (diss-krim-in-AY-shun): Treating a person or group of people unfairly because of their race or gender is known as discrimination. Catholic immigrants faced discrimination when first arriving in the United States.

effigy (EF-i-jee): An effigy is a likeness of a person that might be burned to express anger. Colonists burned a devil effigy to express their hatred for Catholics.

famine (FAM-in): A famine is a severe shortage of food that leads to starvation. Many Irish people died in the potato famine.

migrants (MY-gruhnts): Migrants are workers who must travel from place to place to do their jobs. Many farmworkers are migrants.

poverty (POV-ur-tee): Poverty is the condition of being very poor. Many Irish and Italian people lived in poverty in their homelands.

quotas (KWOH-tuhz): Quotas limit the number of people allowed to do something. In 1924, the U.S. government passed quotas to limit immigration.

Reformation (reh-form-AY-shun): The Reformation refers to the split of the Protestant Church from the Catholic Church. Martin Luther began the Protestant Reformation.

refugees (ref-yoo-JEEZ): Refugees are people who seek safety in a foreign country, especially to avoid war or other dangers. Many Cuban refugees came to the United States after a revolution in Cuba.

SOURCE NOTES

1. James Terence Fisher. *Communion of Immigrants: A History of Catholics in America*. New York, NY: Oxford University Press, 2008. Print. 15.

2. Mary Baba. "Irish Immigrant Families in the Mid-Late 19th Century America." *Yale-New Haven Teachers Institute*. Yale-New Haven Teachers Institute, n.d. Web. 27 June 2018.

3. "In Memory." *Nation of Immigrants*. Angelo A. Paparelli, n.d. Web. 27 June 2018.

4. Peter M. Coan. *Ellis Island Interviews: In Their Own Words*. New York, NY: Facts on File, 1997. Print. 40.

5. Evan Taparata. "The US Has Come a Long Way Since Its First, Highly Restrictive Naturalization Law." *PRI*. Public Radio International, 4 July 2016. Web. 27 June 2018.

6. Alanna Nash. "Gloria and Emilio Estefan Have Rhythm—and Lots of Romance." *AARP*. AARP, n.d. Web. 27 June 2018.

7. Ailsa Fitzwilliam. Personal Interview. 5 May 2018.

8. Carol Kuruvilla. "Pope Francis Urges America to Care for Its Dreamers and Immigrants." *Huffpost*. Oath, 26 Oct. 2017. Web. 27 June 2018.

TO LEARN MORE

Books

MacCarald, Clara. *Irish Immigrants: In Their Shoes*. Mankato, MN: The Child's World, 2018.

McDaniel, Melissa. *Ellis Island*. New York, NY: Children's Press, 2012.

Reilly, Mary-Jo. *Mexico*. New York, NY: Marshall Cavendish Benchmark, 2012.

Web Sites

Visit our Web site for links about Catholic immigrants: childsworld.com/links

Note to Parents, Teachers, and Librarians: We routinely verify our Web links to make sure they are safe and active sites. So encourage your readers to check them out!

INDEX